Air Force One

by Joanne Mattern

Content Consultant
Nanci R. Vargus, Ed.D.
Professor Emeritus, University of Indianapolis

Children's Press®
An Imprint of Scholastic Inc.
New York Toronto London Auckland Sydney
Mexico City New Delhi Hong Kong
Danbury, Connecticut

Library of Congress Cataloging-in-Publication Data
Mattern, Joanne, 1963-
Air Force One/by Joanne Mattern.
     pages cm. — (Rookie read. About American symbols)
Includes bibliographical references and index.
Audience: Ages 3-6.
ISBN 978-0-531-21568-5 (library binding: alk. paper) — ISBN 978-0-531-21841-9 (pbk.: alk. paper)
  1. Air Force One (Presidential aircraft) —Juvenile literature. 2. Presidents—Transportation—United States—Juvenile literature. I. Title.

TL723.M53 2014
387.742088352230973—dc23   2014015031

Produced by Spooky Cheetah Press
Design by Keith Plechaty

© 2015 by Scholastic Inc.

Printed in China 62

SCHOLASTIC, CHILDREN'S PRESS, ROOKIE READ-ABOUT®, and associated logos are trademarks and/or registered trademarks of Scholastic Inc.

1 2 3 4 5 6 7 8 9 10 R 24 23 22 21 20 19 18 17 16 15

Photographs ©: Alamy Images: 8 inset (Everett Collection Inc), 8 bottom (nsf), 31 top (Steven May), 3 bottom (Timm Ziegenthaler/Stocktrek Images), 4 (US Air Force Photo), 12 bottom (Vova Pomortzeff); AP Images/Carolyn Kaster: 3 top left; Department of Defense/U.S. Postal Service: 3 top right; Dreamstime/Christopher Halloran: 20; Getty Images/Ilia Yefimovich: cover; Landov: 23 (Jonathan Ernst/Reuters), 19, 31 bottom (Kevin Lamarque/Reuters); Library of Congress: 11 inset; Media Bakery: 31 center top (Fancy), 31 center bottom (Nigel Riches); Newscom: 12 center (Bruce Murphy/Splash News), 12 top (David McNew/AFP/Getty Images), 28 bottom (Dennis Brack/DanitaDelimont.com), 28 top (Everett Collection); Reuters/Larry Downing: 16; Shutterstock, Inc./Senohrabek: 27; The Image Works: 29 bottom (ArenaPal/Topham), 15 (The White House/Pete Souza), 29 top (TopFoto); U.S. Air Force via Wikipedia: 11 top; White House Photo/Pete Souza via Flickr: 7, 24.

Illustration by Jeffrey Chandler/Art Gecko Studios!

Table of Contents

What Is Air Force One?

Air Force One is a special plane used by the president of the United States. The plane is made just for him.

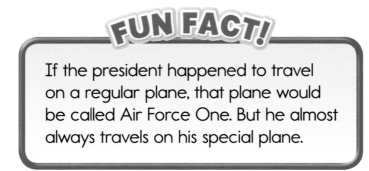

FUN FACT!

If the president happened to travel on a regular plane, that plane would be called Air Force One. But he almost always travels on his special plane.

President Barack Obama and his family return from a trip to South America.

Air Force One takes the president around the country and around the world! No matter where it goes, Air Force One is a symbol of the president and the United States.

FUN FACT!

Some people call Air Force One "the Flying White House."

Harry S. Truman was America's 33rd president.

The History of
Air Force One

Before Harry Truman became president in 1945, most travel was done by train or car. Truman was the first president to travel a lot by airplane. Truman called his plane *The Independence*.

The president travels on his own plane because it is easier and safer than flying on a regular airplane. It is called Air Force One so that **air traffic controllers** don't get it mixed up with other planes.

Dwight D. Eisenhower was the last president to use a plane that wasn't called Air Force One.

Eisenhower's plane was called *The Columbine*.

Dwight D. Eisenhower was the 34th president of the United States.

Each Air Force One plane is used for about 30 years. Then it is replaced. Each plane has special features the president needs.

These photos show how the President's Seal is placed on Air Force One.

Inside Air Force One

Air Force One does not look like other airplanes on the inside. The president has his own office with a desk, computer, telephone, and more. There is also a large meeting room for the president and his staff.

President Obama holds a meeting aboard Air Force One.

16

A chef prepares a meal aboard Air Force One.

Sometimes the president takes long flights to faraway countries. Luckily, Air Force One has bedrooms with couches that turn into beds. The plane also has two kitchens and six bathrooms.

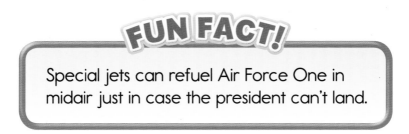

FUN FACT!

Special jets can refuel Air Force One in midair just in case the president can't land.

Members of the **press** also travel with the president. They report on what the president is doing.

President Obama answers questions from reporters.

Air Force One is as tall as a five-story building. It is more than 231 feet (70 meters) long and can fly faster than 700 miles (1,127 kilometers) per hour. That's more than 10 times as fast as most people travel in a car.

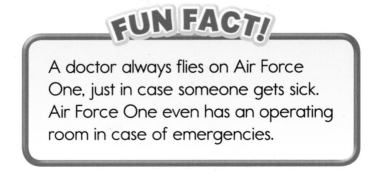

FUN FACT!

A doctor always flies on Air Force One, just in case someone gets sick. Air Force One even has an operating room in case of emergencies.

Super Plane!

The president has to be safe when he is on Air Force One. **Pilots** from the U.S. Air Force are chosen to fly the plane. They are trained to watch for trouble and keep the president safe.

Air Force One is kept at Joint Base Andrews in Maryland.

When it is not flying, Air Force One is kept in a special **hangar** at the airport. Guards watch the plane all day and night. When the president arrives, everything on the plane is ready for him.

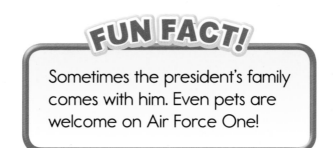

FUN FACT!

Sometimes the president's family comes with him. Even pets are welcome on Air Force One!

Air Force One is ready to fly anytime! It is an important symbol of the United States and the president.

FUN FACT!

Sometimes leaders of other countries fly on Air Force One when they are visiting the president.

American flag

UNITED STATES OF AMERICA

29000

President's Seal

No other airplane in the world looks like Air Force One.

1943
President Franklin D. Roosevelt becomes the first U.S. President to fly to another country.

1953
The name Air Force One is used for the first time.

1948
President Truman begins using a plane called *The Independence*.

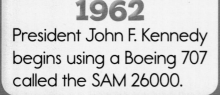

1962
President John F. Kennedy begins using a Boeing 707 called the SAM 26000.

1990
The current Air Force One planes begin flying. These are Boeing 747s called VC-25As. Each plane has a complex telephone and computer system.

2020
A new Air Force One is expected to begin flying.

1959
President Eisenhower is the first president to use a jet as Air Force One.

1972
The SAM 27000 serves as Air Force One. President Richard Nixon is the first president to use this plane.

Passengers eat together in the **dining room**. The plane includes two kitchens.

The **press room** looks a lot like the passenger area on a regular plane.

President's office

The **presidential suite** includes a bedroom, bathroom, and gym.

The plane has 85 phones and 19 TVs on board.

The **control room** is located on level 3. Level 1 of the plane is for storing cargo. Level 2 is the passenger area.

Glossary

air traffic controllers (AIR TRAF-ic kuhn-TROHL-uhrz): people on the ground who control planes in the air

hangar (HANG-ur): building where airplanes are kept

pilots (PYE-luhtz): people who fly airplanes

press (PRESS): people who work for media such as television, radio, newspapers, and the Internet

Index

Facts for Now

Visit this Scholastic Web site for more information on Air Force One:
www.factsfornow.scholastic.com
Enter the keywords **Air Force One**

About the Author

Joanne Mattern is the author of many books for children. She loves writing about history and its special people, places, and things. Joanne lives in New York State with her husband, four children, and numerous pets, and likes to travel as much as she can.